FRANCIS FRITH'S

CHIGWELL

PHOTOGRAPHIC MEMORIES

HUGH PETRIE was born in Holland but brought up from the age of six months in East Finchley, North London, and has a master's degree in history from the University of Essex. He has taught history and museum studies at various English and American universities, and has been heritage officer for the London borough of Barnet for four years. He lives in Highgate with his friends, has an allotment and plays the guitar.

FRANCIS FRITH'S
PHOTOGRAPHIC MEMORIES

CHIGWELL

PHOTOGRAPHIC MEMORIES

HUGH PETRIE

First published in the United Kingdom in 2004 by
Frith Book Company Ltd

Limited Hardback Subscribers Edition Published in 2004
ISBN 1-85937-829-3

Paperback Edition 2004
ISBN 1-85937-830-7

British Library Cataloguing in Publication Data

Francis Frith's Chigwell - Photographic Memories
Hugh Petrie

Frith Book Company Ltd
Frith's Barn, Teffont,
Salisbury, Wiltshire SP3 5QP
Tel: +44 (0) 1722 716 376
Email: info@francisfrith.co.uk
www.francisfrith.co.uk

Printed and bound in Great Britain

Front Cover: **CHIGWELL**, *The Village c1960* C88075t
Frontispiece: **CHIGWELL**, *Brook Parade c1950* C88009

*The colour-tinting is for illustrative purposes only, and is not intended
to be historically accurate*

AS WITH ANY HISTORICAL DATABASE THE FRITH ARCHIVE IS CONSTANTLY
BEING CORRECTED AND IMPROVED AND THE PUBLISHERS WOULD WELCOME
INFORMATION ON OMISSIONS OR INACCURACIES

CONTENTS

FRANCIS FRITH
VICTORIAN PIONEER

FRANCIS FRITH, founder of the world-famous photographic archive, was a complex and multi-talented man. A devout Quaker and a highly successful Victorian businessman, he was philosophical by nature and pioneering in outlook.

By 1855 he had already established a wholesale grocery business in Liverpool, and sold it for the astonishing sum of £200,000, which is the equivalent today of over £15,000,000. Now a very rich man, he was able to indulge his passion for travel. As a child he had pored over travel books written by early explorers, and his fancy and imagination had been stirred by family holidays to the sublime mountain regions of Wales and Scotland. 'What lands of spirit-stirring and enriching scenes and places!' he had written. He was to return to these scenes of grandeur in later years to 'recapture the thousands of vivid and tender memories', but with a different purpose. Now in his thirties, and captivated by the new science of photography, Frith set out on a series of pioneering journeys up the Nile and to the Near East that occupied him from 1856 until 1860.

INTRIGUE AND EXPLORATION

These far-flung journeys were packed with intrigue and adventure. In his life story, written when he was sixty-three, Frith tells of being held captive by bandits, and of fighting 'an awful midnight battle to the very point of surrender with a deadly pack of hungry, wild dogs'. Wearing flowing Arab costume, Frith arrived at Akaba by camel sixty years before Lawrence of Arabia, where he encountered 'desert princes and rival sheikhs, blazing with jewel-hilted swords'.

He was the first photographer to venture beyond the sixth cataract of the Nile. Africa was still the mysterious 'Dark Continent', and Stanley and Livingstone's historic meeting was a decade into the future. The conditions for picture taking confound belief. He laboured for hours in his wicker dark-room in the sweltering heat of the desert, while the volatile chemicals fizzed dangerously in their trays. Back in London he exhibited his photographs and was 'rapturously cheered' by members of the Royal Society. His reputation as a photographer was made overnight.

VENTURE OF A LIFE-TIME

Characteristically, Frith quickly spotted the opportunity to create a new business as a specialist publisher of photographs. He lived in an era of immense and sometimes violent change.

For the poor in the early part of Victoria's reign work was exhausting and the hours long, and people had precious little free time to enjoy themselves. Most had no transport other than a cart or gig at their disposal, and rarely travelled far beyond the boundaries of their own town or village. However, by the 1870s the railways had threaded their way across the country, and Bank Holidays and half-day Saturdays had been made obligatory by Act of Parliament. All of a sudden the working man and his family were able to enjoy days out and see a little more of the world.

With typical business acumen, Francis Frith foresaw that these new tourists would enjoy having souvenirs to commemorate their days out. In 1860 he married Mary Ann Rosling and set out on a new career: his aim was to photograph every city, town and village in Britain. For the next thirty years he travelled the country by train and by pony and trap, producing fine photographs of seaside resorts and beauty spots that were keenly bought by millions of Victorians. These prints were painstakingly pasted into family albums and pored over during the dark nights of winter, rekindling precious memories of summer excursions.

THE RISE OF FRITH & CO

Frith's studio was soon supplying retail shops all over the country. To meet the demand he gathered about him a small team of photographers, and published the work of independent artist-photographers of the calibre of Roger Fenton and Francis Bedford. In order to gain some understanding of the scale of Frith's business one only has to look at the catalogue issued by Frith & Co in 1886: it runs to some 670 pages, listing not only many thousands of views of the British Isles but also many photographs of most European countries, and China, Japan, the USA and Canada - note the sample page shown on page 9 from the hand-written Frith & Co ledgers recording the pictures. By 1890 Frith had created the greatest specialist photographic publishing company in the world, with over 2,000 sales outlets - more than the combined number that Boots and WH Smith have today! The picture on the next page shows the Frith & Co display board at Ingleton in the Yorkshire Dales (left of window). Beautifully constructed with a mahogany frame and gilt inserts, it could display up to a dozen local scenes.

POSTCARD BONANZA

The ever-popular holiday postcard we know today took many years to develop. In 1870 the Post Office issued the first plain cards, with a pre-printed stamp on one face. In 1894 they allowed other publishers' cards to be sent through the mail with an attached adhesive halfpenny stamp. Demand grew rapidly, and in 1895 a new size of postcard was permitted called the court card, but there was little room for illustration. In 1899, a year after Frith's death, a new card measuring 5.5 x 3.5 inches became the standard format, but it was not until 1902 that the divided back came into being, so that the address and message could be on one face and a full-size illustration on the other. Frith & Co were in the vanguard of postcard development: Frith's sons Eustace and Cyril continued their father's monumental task, expanding the number of views offered to the public and recording more and more places in Britain, as the coasts and countryside were opened up to mass travel.

Francis Frith had died in 1898 at his villa in Cannes, his great project still growing. The archive he created continued in business for another seventy years. By 1970 it contained over a third of a million pictures showing 7,000 British towns and villages.

FRANCIS FRITH'S LEGACY

Frith's legacy to us today is of immense significance and value, for the magnificent archive of evocative photographs he created provides a unique record of change in the cities, towns and villages throughout Britain over a century and more. Frith and his fellow studio photographers revisited locations many times down the years to update their views, compiling for us an enthralling and colourful pageant of British life and character.

We are fortunate that Frith was dedicated to recording the minutiae of everyday life. For it is this sheer wealth of visual data, the painstaking chronicle of changes in dress, transport, street layouts, buildings, housing, engineering and landscape that captivates us so much today. His remarkable images offer us a powerful link with the past and with the lives of our ancestors.

THE VALUE OF THE ARCHIVE TODAY

Computers have now made it possible for Frith's many thousands of images to be accessed almost instantly. Frith's images are increasingly used as visual resources, by social historians, by researchers into genealogy and ancestry, by architects and town planners, and by teachers involved in local history projects.

In addition, the archive offers every one of us an opportunity to examine the places where we and our families have lived and worked down the years. Highly successful in Frith's own era, the archive is now, a century and more on, entering a new phase of popularity. Historians consider the Francis Frith Collection to be of prime national importance. It is the only archive of its kind remaining in private ownership. Francis Frith's archive is now housed in an historic timber barn in the beautiful village of Teffont in Wiltshire. Its founder would not recognize the archive office as it is today. In place of the many thousands of dusty boxes containing glass plate negatives and an all-pervading odour of photographic chemicals, there are now ranks of computer screens. He would be amazed to watch his images travelling round the world at unimaginable speeds through internet lines.

The archive's future is both bright and exciting. Francis Frith, with his unshakeable belief in making photographs available to the greatest number of people, would undoubtedly approve of what is being done today with his lifetime's work. His photographs depicting our shared past are now bringing pleasure and enlightenment to millions around the world a century and more after his death.

CHIGWELL
AN INTRODUCTION

THIS IS A COLLECTION of pictures taken by Frith photographers of various views and locations in and around the Chigwell area. Chigwell is famed for its public house called the King's Head. The reason for this is simply that it was used as the model for the Maypole in 'Barnaby Rudge' by Charles Dickens: he described it as 'an old building, with more gable ends than a lazy man would care to count on a sunny day; huge zigzag chimneys, out of which it seemed as though even smoke could not choose but come in more than naturally fantastic shapes, imparted to it in its tortuous progress; and vast stables, gloomy, ruinous, and empty'.

We have been quite liberal with our definition of the Chigwell area. It was not the original intention of Frith's, a postcard company, to produce histories (though they did photograph historical buildings), but to produce picturesque views. However, these postcards have become a

NOAK HILL, *St Thomas' Chapel and the School 1908* 59852

historical source; and, like many other sources in local history and genealogy, this slight inconsistency is a part of their charm. This history is not intended as a corporation and parish history; we leave that to the Victoria County Histories. The area of the photographs selected is a coherent one, and to younger locals it is clearly defined as being 'very nearly a part of London', by virtue of being on the London side of the M25. To older eyes we are looking at a small portion of south-west Essex trapped by a transport policy and the local authority act of 1963. For many of us Londoners, and East Enders in particular, Loughton, Theydon Bois, Chigwell, and beyond was the countryside. I first visited the area with my brothers, camping in Epping Forest in the late 1970s, when you still could (but no fires were allowed). Then, as now, and since the times of the medieval kings, this south-western corner of Essex and Epping Forest in particular has been an area of recreation.

Until the early 19th century, much of the western part of the parish of Chigwell, that is Buckhurst Hill, and the adjacent areas we have included like Woodford and Loughton, were within the forest itself. Epping and Hainault Forest are truly ancient, and are nearly all that still remains of a much greater forest which stretched from the Wash to the Thames. Epping Forest is the largest concentration of hornbeam in England.

Historically speaking, many of the stories about the Forest are fanciful. It is said to be the death place of Boudicca and her daughters from poisoned berries, and some have bravely suggested that Robin Hood lived in the woods. Less fanciful is the tradition of free hunting, which was granted to the people of London by Henry III in 1226 - but only on Easter Monday. This may explain the meaning of the names of public houses like the Bald Faced Hind (see below). It certainly became a great occasion even into the 19th century, and during the rest of the year various kings and queens hunted here. To them these forests were the Royal Forests of Essex. However, by the 18th century the royal family only hunted here occasionally. By the 19th century, the wood was being severely reduced through clearing and enclosure, and its acreage was reduced by half. Local people had the right to lop wood for winter fuel, provided the right was exercised by midnight on 11 November. According to the Willingale family history page (http://www.willingale.org), a landowner tried to trick the loppers with a supper at the Kings Head in Loughton on the same day, hoping that the men would lose track of time and lose the right; but he was out-foxed by one of the loppers, Thomas Willingale, who realised what was happening and managed to lop a single branch before the allotted hour.

Later there was a public outcry over the enclosures, particularly in London. The Corporation of London, as owners of land in the Forest, took the various lords of the manor concerned to the Court of Chancery, and this court declared that the enclosures made from 1851 to 1874 had been illegal. In 1878 the woods were handed over to the control of the Corporation of London, who run it still.

Just east of the Forest we have a line of conurbation, a consequence of the clearance, much of which dates from the arrival of the railway in the 1850s and 1860s. The railway lines, reaching as far north as Epping by 1865, brought cheaper fuel, and more comfortable and quicker communications with London than the horse-drawn omnibuses and coaches. The result was new houses and shops in areas such as Snaresbrook (a name taken from the railway station), Woodford, the east end of the ancient parish of Chigwell, and Buckhurst Hill. This spur of London was ready to capture the Forest itself, and would have done so but for the City of London's action described above. Epping Forest became a wedge of fields and woodland running from as far north as Theydon Bois south to Snaresbrook, separating the areas of Walthamstow and Chingford in the west for ever from Woodford and Loughton to the east. The population increased, and by 1895 areas like Buckhurst Hill, for example, became urban authorities in their own right. Far to the south of Chigwell, the construction of the railway in 1839 had led to a great increase in the populations of Romford and Ilford during the 19th century. But these growing conurbations did not impinge on the area represented in this book until the 20th century. Ilford's population rose from around ten thousand in the 1890s to more than a hundred and seventy thousand by the 1950s, and now only Hainault Forest separates Chigwell Row from the London Borough of Redbridge.

By the 1900s it looked as if Chigwell was going to be developed in much the same way as Woodford, Ilford, and Romford. In 1903 the construction of the Woodford and Ilford loop line (the present line) provided a train service able to cope with the large-scale supply of building material for such new developments. The London General Omnibus Company, already with a garage in Seven Kings by 1913, was running services which made Chigwell (and areas even further east, such as Havering-atte-Bower and Abridge) 'commutable' by 1917. It was possible to catch the 'bus to jobs in Stratford, and with connections with the fast railway services from Ilford and Romford, the City could now be

LOUGHTON, *Winter in Epping Forest c1960* L106033

reached in just over an hour, if the journey was timed right. By the 1920s the motorcar particularly threatened to bring more housing to the area, which could be built by developers of more affluent suburbs.

The reason why urbanisation around Chigwell and further east was not rapid after the railways came is simple. Many of the local landowners were not prepared to sell off their homes, massive estates, and farms straight away. After all, they provided a country living within easy reach of the centre of political power, London. The First World War delayed matters further, bringing to a halt any building projects all over England. After the First World War, however, things began again to favour the developers. The world economy took a down-turn, and with the rising cost of servants (who were necessary to keep these very large houses in good order), more and more landowners began to offer their estates on the open market. Advertisements in 'The Times' show that some of these estates were being sold off as piecemeal building land. In the 1930s London Transport announced that it intended to run the Central Line round the loop line to Chigwell. Just before the Second World War we do see some building, with shopping parades like Brookside Parade, and some suburban-style domestic roads. It is interesting to compare The Bowls in Chigwell Row with Chigwell Hall, a much larger building. Built within fifty years of each other, the former was redeveloped into flats in the 1960s, while the latter became a police sports club. But it is

interesting to consider what would have happened if Chigwell Hall and its estate had been developed. The village would certainly have lost its separate identity from the general conurbation of London, one of the key objectives of the Green Belt laws of the late 1930s. This successful legislation led Sir Nicolas Pevsner to describe Chigwell in the 1950s as the first real village on the way out north-east of London. In November 1947 the tube line was opened at Chigwell.

The new Green Belt, first established in 1937, along with the Town and Country Planning Acts of 1944 and 1947, gave local people the necessary leverage to stop wholesale redevelopment of villages and farms. The result is a pocket of countryside reaching several miles as far as the outer reach of this survey (the M25), with still picturesque villages such as Chigwell, Theydon Bois, Havering-atte-Bower, and Abridge. This is why these images are so important as a record. As well as recording those villages, it also brings together photographs from the more developed western areas. Most of the images are from the 1950s and 1960s, with a few Edwardian and 1920s images. What is remarkable is how little has changed. Compare, for example, the images of Chigwell village in the 1920s with those of the 1950s and 1960s. But enough has changed to encourage curiosity. These images show the area when Green Belt legislation and the Town and Country Planning Act were first established; they could hardly be more pertinent as we now remember the success of these acts 60 years later.

CHIGWELL

CHIGWELL, *The King's Head c1950* C88011

The Kings Head is an ancient public house. The timber-framed building is, according to Pevsner, 17th-century, with considerable additions made in 1901. Photographs from the 1900s show the outside as having been plastered, which was stripped away by the 1920s to reveal a splendid half-timbered front.

CHIGWELL
*The King's Head,
the Gardens 1925*
78725

The Kings Head was the model for the Maypole in Dickens's 'Barnaby Rudge'. Although there is a Maypole Inn at Chigwell Row (see below), it was quite clear to residents of Chigwell itself that Dickens's description was of their own Kings Head. Later, when cornered, Dickens admitted that he used a writer's licence, combining a description of the one house in the location of the other.

CHIGWELL, *The King's Head, the Gardens c1955* C88014

By 1713 the Chester Room of the Kings Head was being used by the Court of Attachments of Waltham Forest, which met to decide on minor disputes. Stephen Pewsy, in 'Chigwell and Loughton: A Pictorial History', says that the gateway to the pub, demolished in modern times to make way for the motorcars, even had a small cell to confine miscreants.

▼ **CHIGWELL,** *The King's Head, the Interior c1954* C88016

In April 1941 the house suffered some damage during an air raid, but it was in good enough repair to provide Winston Churchill, then the local MP, and his wife with luncheon whilst touring the district during the General Election of 1945. The interior is at present being refurbished.

► **CHIGWELL**
The Village 1925 78724

This is very much the picturesque Chigwell that Dickens knew. It is easy to see what he meant when he invited his friend, and later biographer, Forster to visit the area with the words: 'Chigwell, my dear fellow, is the greatest place in the world'.

▲ **CHIGWELL,** *The Bakery c1955* C88006

Guyden's Bakery (left) is a long-time landmark of the village; the front is 19th-century, but the building behind dates from the 18th century. At the time of this photograph, John Delaney ran the shop. It is now the Bluebell Restaurant, a location in the BBC documentary 'Essex Wives'.

▶ **CHIGWELL**
The Bakery c1965
C88146

Here we have an almost identical view some ten years later. One of the great advantages of the Frith Collection is that the photographers often went back to the same locations, which provides us with subtle degrees of change. Here the Bakery has clearly been refurbished.

▼ **CHIGWELL,** *The Village 1925* 78723
This next group of photographs, this one along with C88015 and C88075, again shows gradual change. At this time the stores (centre) were run by George Watts, and the bakery by George Hayden. Notice the complete lack of road traffic.

▶ **CHIGWELL**
The Village c1960
C88075

This last photograph in the chronological sequence shows us the stores when they were still run by the Martin family. Notice that the shop front has been changed. Electoral records show that a Shirish and Jyoti Ghandi ran the shop from about 1963.

CHIGWELL
The Village c1955 C88015

Here we can see the shop at the time when it was run by
Leonard and Violet Martin. In those days, local shopkeepers
arranged to have an early closing day. In the case of
Chigwell, early closing was Thursday.

CHIGWELL
1955 C88104

These weatherboard houses were very common throughout Essex and Middlesex during the 18th and 19th centuries. After the great fire (1666), the use of wood was not common in the London area, and as a material it more common in the countryside. Because of the spread of London, houses like this have become rare in Middlesex.

CHIGWELL, *The Grammar School 1925* 78726

Samuel Harsnett, eventually Archbishop of York, was Vicar of St Mary's from 1597 to 1605. Being fond of the parish, Harsnett established two schools in Chigwell: an English school, and a Latin school. It was the latter institution that became today's private school.

CHIGWELL
Harsnetts 1925
78721

Opposite the school is Harsnetts. It was bought by Samuel Harsnett in around 1627, and he leased it for £60 a year. It has been variously used by the school over the centuries, and became a boarding house for the smaller boys in 1896, when it was given its present name.

CHIGWELL, *The Vicarage 1925* 78727

Apart from Samuel Harsnett, other Vicars have included Roger Fenton (1565-1616), a writer and theologian best known for his translations for the Authorized Version of the Bible. He was Vicar of St Mary's until his death in 1616.

CHIGWELL
The Church of St Mary the Virgin 1925 78728

This is the Anglican parish church of Chigwell. Parts of the fabric of the church are Norman, from the 12th century. The population of the parish increased from 1,351 in 1801 to 2,059 in 1841, making the small medieval church unsuitable. The extensions were designed by Sir Arthur Blomfield and completed in 1886, and by and large this is the church we see today. Outside is the war memorial; it was unveiled by Sir Francis Lloyd, with a guard of honour from the school cadet force, on 6 November 1921.

CHIGWELL
The Boys' Grammar School c1955 C88013

By the time this photograph was taken the school had facilities for 350 boys, but originally this hall of 1629 held only a handful of local boys. It would have still been a new school when William Penn went there at the age of 11 in the 1650s. He went on to found the settlement from which the state of Pennsylvania takes its name.

CHIGWELL, *The Boys' Grammar School c1955* C88060

This is New Hall, built to designs by Rex Hunter; the foundation stone was laid in June 1929. It was originally called the Tercentenary Hall, but as this is a bit of mouthful, it quickly became renamed New Hall by the boys. It was a part of a great expansion of the school during the 1930s.

CHIGWELL
The School, the Swallow Library
c1960 C88106

Canon Swallow was headmaster of the school between 1876 and 1912. He oversaw the school's conversion from a local grammar school into a private school. This library with its curious dome (left) was dedicated to the memory of Canon Swallow, and was designed to have a capacity for 10,000 books.

CHIGWELL, *West Hatch School c1960* C88100

According to Nicolas Pevsner, West Hatch Technical School was built between 1957 and 1967 to designs by H Connolly. It was built on the site of the Royal Eastern Counties Institution for Mental Defectives (women and girls), a large hospital.

► **CHIGWELL**
The Village School c1955
C88025

There had been a National (Anglican) school in Chigwell since the 1830s, and by the 1870s Chigwell had a school board. The shape of the school shown here was the result of extensions made during the 1890s and 1900s.

◄ **CHIGWELL**
The Village School c1925 C88057

Despite popular opposition, the school had to be demolished in June 1970. The woodwork was so diseased that it had be burned, and all that remains is, apparently, a single hall.

▲ **CHIGWELL,** *A Meadow c1965* C88065

The spire in the background is that of St Mary's, and this view has not changed. The meadow behind the present rectory, now over-run with rabbits, shows how well the village has been preserved, with most of the developments to the south and west. We can see why Pevsner described Chigwell as the first true village north east out of London.

◄**CHIGWELL**
*Brook House Farm
c1955* C88032

This is an ancient farmhouse built in the 17th century; note the six twisted brick central chimneys. This was not the first building here, and the farm is known to have existed in the 15th century. The building was demolished in the early 1960s.

▶ **CHIGWELL**
Spanbrook Flats
c1965 C88212

This is the building
that replaced
Brookhouse Farm
(see C88032, page 27).
It is a modest
example of a common
enough style, with
vaguely Corbusier
elements. This shot
was taken shortly
before the first
residents moved in.

◀ **CHIGWELL**
Brook Parade c1950
C88009

Just before the Second
World War there were a
number of residential
streets established
around Chigwell, and
more were to have been
built. These shops with
flats above were built in
c1938, and provide most
of the retail space for the
village. In the distance is
Brookhouse Farm.

▲ **CHIGWELL,** *Grange Farm Camp Holiday Centre c1960* C88073

Grange Farm was offered on the market as building land in 1935, but it was purchased in 1938 by the London Parochial Charities as a campsite for the children of families living in the East End of London who could not afford a sea-side holiday.

◀ **CHIGWELL**
The Grange Farm Centre c1960 C88090

The centre was in use with temporary structures shortly after the war, but was formally built between 1950 and 1951 as a part of the Festival of Britain. The designs for the 107 acres of land included huts for 400 boys and girls, and a further 200 could be accommodated under canvas. Tennis courts and bowling greens and other sports facilities, which were funded by Chigwell Urban District, were made available for local people.

CHIGWELL
Grange Farm Centre
c1965 C88121

The centre was opened on
12 July 1951 by the then
Princess Elizabeth, now the
Queen, accompanied by
Winston Churchill, the local
MP. As the young princess
said at the centre's opening,
'No community, especially
that which lived its daily life
in and among the streets of
a city, could thrive without
open air and exercise'.

CHIGWELL
Grange Farm, the Chapel c1965 C88210

The chapel was built to designs by Kenneth Lindy
& Partners. They had the almost impossible task of providing
for a congregation which number in the hundreds in the
summer, but with only a small plot. Their solution was to use
side walls which could be folded away, thus allowing for
semi-outdoor services.

CHIGWELL
The Disabled Persons' Unit,
Grange Farm Centre c1965 C88126

The centre was of particular importance to London's
disabled as a resort. The Winged Fellowship used it as a
centre for respite care and holidays for the disabled. Most
particularly, in 1964 the centre was established as a place
that provided riding lessons for the wheelchair-bound.
This centre had grown from the work of Norah Jacques at
Forest Lodge Riding School in the late 1950s.

33

CHIGWELL
*The Swimming Pool at
Grange Farm Centre
c1960* C88022

By the 1960s, with
improving living standards
making the original purpose
of the centre largely
redundant, the centre was
mostly a local amenity.
The swimming pool was
one of the main features of
the centre, providing for the
Chigwell area. It was
financed with money from
the King George Jubilee
Trust fund, and is
remembered with great
affection locally.

▼ **CHIGWELL,** *The Swimming Pool at Grange Farm Centre c1960* C88088

The swimming pool existed until 1973, according to Stephen Pewsy in 'Chigwell and Loughton: A Pictorial History'. Then the centre became a camp site, and finally closed altogether in 1984. The whole site is currently under redevelopment with the inclusion of some homes for the disabled.

◀**CHIGWELL**
The Golf Club c1955
C88051

The course was built to designs by Hawtree & Taylor in 1924 on 99 acres of land, and the first games were being played by April the next year. Officially opened in October of the same year, the rounds were played by Lord Lambourne, Lord Lieutenant of Essex, and the renowned Harry Vardon of Totteridge Golf Club, Hertfordshire. It is still a critically acclaimed and well-kept course.

▲ **CHIGWELL,** *The Golf Club c1965* C88214

The club house was rebuilt shortly before this photograph was taken. According to the club's website, it has in recent times hosted national events such as the English Girls' Championship in 1999, as well as the Essex County Championships the year before.

◄ **CHIGWELL**
The Hall c1965 88151

Chigwell Hall dominates the land behind the churchyard of St Mary's. It was built in 1876 to designs by Norman Shaw, his only house in the area. It is now a Grade II listed building.

CHIGWELL
The Hall c1955
C88053

This is an ancient name for an essentially late 19th-century building. The name relates to the manor of Chigwell Hall, which at one time belonged to Earl Harold, later King Harold, of Battle of Hastings fame.

CHIGWELL, *The Hall, the Cricket Ground c1955* C88052

Chigwell Hall is a sports centre for Number 5 district of the Metropolitan Police. It has had a number of different occupants; at one time it was the home of A Savill, who was responsible for much of the area's redevelopment (see C88109, page 39).

CHIGWELL
Roding Lane c1960
C88109

Roding Lane takes its name from the River Roding, which it crosses at White Bridge. According to Stephen Pewsy in 'Chigwell and Loughton: A Pictorial History', the lane was originally a path which connected Buckhurst and Chigwell. It was redeveloped as Chigwell New Road by A Savill in 1906.

GWELL, *Coolgardie Avenue c1960* C88101

road is typical of the building projects that were conducted after the Second World War. Ordnance Survey maps show t was built on the site of an older road, New Barn Road, whose path had run across the present road, but which was ked by the railway of 1903.

39

▼ **CHIGWELL,** *Courtland Drive c1965* C88134

This road was built on the site of Rookery Farm, and an ancient footpath still runs through this estate which was used to service the farm. The style here is mock-Tudor, but unlike elsewhere around London, these houses were built in about 1938 with a degree of individuality. The houses overlook the fields.

► **CHIGWELL**
Home Farm c1960
C88108

Until the 1960s, farming was the most important economic activity in the area. Home Farm is one of the few farms still working within the M25; during the 1960s it was run by Bert and Myrtle Padfield.

◄ **CHIGWELL**
Manor Hall c1955
C88056

Manor Hall was built shortly after 1935 as a dance hall at a time when a number of residential estates were being built south of Manor Road. Manor Hall has since become a popular banqueting hall. It has been owned by the same family, the Spouse family, since 1946.

► **CHIGWELL**
The Bald Hind Public House c1955 C88049

This is an Edwardian building, but there has been a house of this name here since at least the 18th century. Some believe that the sign came about because of the custom of public hunts at Easter. A tame deer, decorated with ribbons, was hunted, and in lieu of a piece of the carcase, participants took hair from the front of the face—thus the bald face in the pub's name.

CHIGWELL ROW

CHIGWELL ROW,
All Saints' Church c1965 C240063

The first rector of the church was the Rev Richard Lawrence in 1860, but the church was built a little later in 1867. Chigwell Row developed during the 19th century: a number of houses were built at the edge of a small stretch of green or waste, which in those days constituted the road. During the second half of the century, probably starting with the new Maypole, this waste was built on, effectively creating two rows of buildings ending at the Two Brewers.

CHIGWELL ROW
The View from the Church Tower c1955
C240007

Looking down from the tower of the church, we see the Maypole public house (c1860s). Dickens first encountered the house on his many excursions he made away from London when not writing. For this he may well have used the horse-drawn omnibus service to Whitechapel that was provided by William Powling.

GWELL ROW, *The Maypole c1965* C240034

s not the original house or even the location of the original house, which until the 1970s was situated behind the nt building. However, the house had been made very popular because of Dickens's 'Barnaby Rudge'; also, a convenient bus service from Ilford station was being run by Powling's widow. Therefore a rebuild was essential to cope with the rade. Ironically, the old Maypole was obscured from view from the road, and the picturesque pond in front of it was ed. Chigwell Row's most famous former resident was Shillibeer, the man who brought the idea of the omnibus, a ge with a fixed fare running a fixed route, from Parish to London in 1829.

43

▼ **CHIGWELL ROW,** *The Two Brewers c1955* C240002

This is the second public house of the village, and a lot less famous than the Maypole. It was originally a beer house, which was established as the village grew. Here we see it in its original condition before the first extensions were done in the second half of the 20th century. At the time of writing, it was undergoing further refurbishments and extensions.

► **CHIGWELL ROW**
The Village School and the Common c1955
C240001

Some small boy has 'tagged' his initials ('CP') and the year into the brick wall, but as this was 1878, we are probably too late for any suitable punishment. There was already a National (Anglican) village school, but this is a later British (non-conformist) school. It was newly built when CP made his mark.

44

The Girl Guides'
Hut c1965 C240067

This was an important 56-acre camping ground for the Guide and Brownie groups in East London, as this part of the countryside was easily reached by train, especially with electrification in the late 1940s. This hut's name, Jubilee House, dates it to about 1935, the Jubilee of George V.

GWELL ROW
lands Farm
55 C240012

pretty house sits
away from the
, and is the
len's house for the
Guides Camping
nd. It is built on
riginal line of
lings which ended
the first Maypole
with its pond and
n, which
tituted the
well Row which
ens knew.

CHIGWELL ROW
Manor Road c1955 C240003

In the centre of the picture are the now demolished (c1958)
Marden Cottages, the clapperboard houses.

CHIGWELL ROW
The Main Road and Marden Close c1965 C240027

This view was taken about ten years later than C240003 from a
similar position (the semi-detached houses are out of the picture
to the left where they should be). The garage to the right has
recently been demolished, and in the distance is the
Two Brewers.

► **CHIGWELL ROW**
Manor Road c1955
C240004

The shop on the left is Morgan's, selling confectionery, and the shop is still an old-fashioned confectioner's just as Morgan would have remembered it. These buildings were built on the wastes in front of the original Chigwell Row in c1880. F Harman & Co, whose sign we can just make out on the gate next to Morgan's, were builders, and this was their yard.

◄ **CHIGWELL ROW**
Lambourne Road c1965 C240053

Like Morgan's the confectioner's (C240004), this shop (left), a post office and grocer's run by Pardey & Johnson, was built at the end of the 19th century. At this point it is easy to see how the row of shops has been built forward onto the waste.

▲ **CHIGWELL ROW,** *The Bowls c1965* C240025

For a while the Chigwell area became popular with the richer sort, who built larger houses, but their time was often short-lived. The Bowls flats were built by T A Clark Holdings Ltd between 1967 and 1968 on the site of a larger house of the same name built in 1915.

◀**CHIGWELL ROW**
A View towards Hainault Forest c1955
C240020

Hainault Forest was once the property of Barking Abbey. In the 18th century, Daniel Day established the Fairlop Fair there, with a feast for his friends and tenants. In the 19th century it was the home of Dido, a homeless folk medicine-man renowned for his herbal cures. The forest was considerably reduced in size by clearance in the 1850s for farmland, and has subsequently become parkland.

CHIGWELL ROW
The Lake, Hainault Forest c1965 C240030

This is the pond which is marked on mid 19th-century Ordnance
Survey maps as Sheep Water. It is most likely that this is where
sheep being driven up to London from Essex and Suffolk were
dipped and watered here, hence its name.

CHIGWELL ROW
The Beehive c1965 C240056

The sign was an easy one to put up: all that was required was
simply a common skep-style hive to be placed outside the house.
But by the 18th century it was used as an icon to indicate
industriousness among the more puritan. This house has been
around since at least 1770, and the present house (now the
Camelot) was a rebuild of 1928.

EAST OF CHIGWELL – HAVERING-ATTE-BOWER AND ABRIDGE

ABRIDGE
The Mill near Passingford Bridge c1960
A160610

There have been a number of different mills on this location, including a windmill at one time. This incarnation of the mill is at least 18th-century. Its water wheel was removed in the 1930s.

▼ **ABRIDGE,** *The Village c1960* A106020

The Malsters Arms (left), originally a beer-house, is still very much the same, although it has expanded into the cottages to the left. The rather splendid bay-windowed building on the right at the bottom of Hoe Lane is The Poplars. It was built some time before 1872, and it was demolished and replaced with council housing in about 1965.

◀**ABRIDGE**
The Village c1960
A106012

We have turned the corner we saw in photograph A106020. The view is much the same today, with Gould's Cottages (c1840) on the left-hand side. On the right the weatherboard house is Retreat House, for much of the 20th century a post office, and now much extended.

RIDGE, *The Market Place c1960* A106016

White Hart building (right) dates from the 1880s, but the establishment is much older, being mentioned in a list of s of the 1720s. A cattle fair was held in June at Abridge from the 18th century to the 1870s.

◄**ABRIDGE**
The Market Place c1960
A106017

The Blue Boar, the building on the left with the two columns, is mid 19th-century, and was probably built to sell the products of the Anchor Brewery, which became the Abridge Brewery and finally a store for the Whitbread company. However, it is mentioned on the same 18th-century list as The White Hart.

NOAK HILL
*St Thomas' Chapel and
the School 1908* 59852

The school (left) is still there,
but it has been much
refurbished, and the
picturesque porch and
chimney pots have not stood
the test of time. Its nice to
see that it is still being used
as a school. Pevsner describes
St Thomas' as 'the only
building of note'; it was
built in c1841 to designs by
G Smith.

NOAK HILL
Noak Hill Road
1908 59854

The bend in the road allows us to place this view quite accurately: the building we see here was once next door to the present Rose Cottages. According to local knowledge, the house was at one time used as a sweet shop and post office; it has, however, long since been demolished.

HAVERING-ATTE-BOWER, *The Village 1908* 59845

The house on the right where the lady is standing is now called Ruskin House. But this view is very much changed. The building on the left of the picture is not almshouses, as might be thought from the row of doors; rather, they are early 19th-century agricultural labourers' tenements called Elizabeth Row, and now demolished. The Red Lion beyond Ruskin House has also gone.

HAVERING-ATTE-BOWER
The Stocks and Whipping Post 1908 59849

There is still a stocks and whipping post at Havering-atte-Bower, and there has been since at least the 17th century, when they were destroyed by a mob. They have stood on this location, at the edge of the green on Broxhill Road, since about 1829. Those that stand today date from the 1960s, and are a singular attraction for visitors; the ones we see here were actually used.

59

HAVERING-ATTE-BOWER
The Orange Tree 1908
59851

This pub on the road to Havering-atte-Bower has retained much of its shape, although it is now brightly painted. Although having an orange tree would have been a great attraction, and the use of such curiosities to attract people to inns were common from the 17th to the beginning of the 20th century, it is not likely that this was the origins of this house. The name the Orange Tree was a political statement of loyalty to William of Orange during the revolution of 1688.

▼ **HAVERING-ATTE-BOWER,** *Havering Hall 1908* 60678

This house was built by W Pemberton Barnes to replace an earlier house built in the 18th century. In 1924 the estate had 1,552 acres, 400 of which were parkland. The Havering manor was a crown manor from the time of Harold, of Hastings fame, until 1828.

▶ **HAVERING-ATTE-BOWER**
Bedfords 1908 60680

Bedfords was rebuilt in 1771, and much altered by Charles Barber between 1865 and 1867. In 1922 the estate was described as having 125 acres of woodland and park, and being 300 feet above sea level with fine views across to Kent. The house we see here was demolished in 1959.

◄ **HAVERING-ATTE-BOWER**
Bedfords, the Lodge 1910
62774

This lodge survived the demolition of the house to form an entrance to a public park established after the death of H J Stone, when his wife sold the land to Romford Urban District Council in the 1930s. This lodge survived until the early 1970s.

► **HAVERING-ATTE-BOWER**
Havering Court 1910 62775

Originally the house was called Cromwell House, and at the time of the photograph it was known as Rose Court; it became known as Havering Court later. Built in 1858 by John Galding, it was greatly enlarged during the 1890s. It was very much damaged by fire in the 1930s and was left derelict.

HAVERING-ATTE-BOWER
Pyrgo Park 1910 62782

This house was built in the 1850s. Parts of the estate, some 571
acres, were being offered as building plots by 1920, and were sold
to developers by 1935. Pre-war Green Belt laws enabled Essex
County Council to block planning permission, and they acquired
the site in 1937 and demolished the house in 1940.

HAVERING-ATTE-BOWER
Bower House, the South Façade c1965 H42008

This house was built in 1792 for John Baynes. It is a modest
Palladian house designed by Henry Flitcroft, his first commission.
The wings are additions of the 1800s. When this photograph was
taken, Bower House was the home of the Ford Marketing Institute.

WEST OF CHIGWELL – LOUGHTON AND WOODFORD

HIGH BEACH
Near the Robin Hood Public House 1911 63887

Epping Forest's pleasant vistas and the opportunities it offers for a quiet escape from the busy troubles of London are the attractions that brought people here – and no doubt the romantic name of the Robin Hood Tavern (built in Victorian times) helped.

LOUGHTON
Winter in Epping Forest c1960 L106033

This charming winter scene is typical of Epping Forest. However, despite Victorian references to Robin Hood, the Epping Forest of the 18th century was genuinely a remote place and the haunt of highwaymen like Sixteen String Jack (c1760), who evaded the hangman for many years.

THEYDON BOIS, *The Pond and the Green c1955* T111004

The village of Theydon Bois Green has existed since the 18th century; it constituted the parish's only real settlement. The railway, which extended to here and Epping in 1865, brought further development.

THEYDON BOIS
The Green c1955 T111006

The building to the right of this image is the Bull, known as the Bull's Head in the 17th century. To the middle left is the Clockhouse, built in the 1920s; at this date it was a shop owned by G E Bridgeland. The character of the area has been kept intact through the dedicated work of the Village Preservation Society, which was founded in 1943.

▼ **LOUGHTON,** *The Church of St John the Baptist 1923* 73924

Built to designs by Sir Sidney Smirk in 1846, this church was much enlarged in 1877, as the population had doubled between 1851 and 1871. It is not the original church, which is St Nicholas' Church.

► **LOUGHTON**
Station Road c1955
L106008

Lopping Hall, the building with the clock tower on the right-hand side, was named in honour of the commoners' rites to cut or lop wood (see introduction). There is a foundation stone that declares that the hall was opened by the Lord Mayor of London in September 1883.

LOUGHTON
The High Road and the War Memorial c1960 L106042

At the end of the High Road we can just see the war memorial (left), which was erected in memory of the 92 men of the district who lost their lives during the First World War. It was unveiled by Lord Lambourne, then Lord Lieutenant of Essex.

BUCKHURST HILL
The Congregational Church 1923 73931

This church was built in 1874 at a cost of £6,000. From that time the congregation expanded to over 160 in the 1950s, but the church was never full. During the 1960s and 70s the congregation declined, and much of the church was demolished and replaced by retirement flats. However, unlike many places this landmark still stands tall, as its splendid tower remains.

▶ **WOODFORD**
The George Hotel 1921
70105

The George (centre left) was formerly called the Horns. It is an 18th-century building with many 19th-century additions. As an institution, its earliest incarnation can be traced at least to 1625. It was the location for the meetings of the local vestry, but the inn fell into disrepute by the 1830s. It is supposed to be haunted by at least two ghosts.

◄ **WOODFORD GREEN**
A Farmyard 1904 53059

Woodford Green was well developed when this photograph was taken. The location is most likely Monkham Farm, as the photographer had probably taken a picture of the big house of the same name, and had chosen this as a picturesque view. At this time the farm was managed by Charles Schwier.

▲ **WOODFORD GREEN**
Salway Hill 1921 70109

This is Elfrida Parade. George Gray & Sons
(the second awning from the left) had
been trading there since at least 1912, and
probably even earlier. The motorbuses
reached the area by 1912, servicing
districts not covered by the tram system;
they had only just become a reliable form
of transportation.

▲ WOODFORD GREEN
High Road c1950 W132019

This view includes a number of shops which were established by the 1920s, including Chapman & Harris the butcher's (third from the right) and Mavers the hairdresser's (near right). The rather fun spectacles on the left of the picture belong to F W Dadd & Partners, ophthalmic opticians, of The Terrace, a stretch of shops built in the 1880s.

◀ *detail from W132019*

WOODFORD BRIDGE
High Road c1950
W479013

Much of this scene had not changed since before the war. The post office (near right) was run by F S Mowlam in the 1950s. Further on we see the gabled end of the White Hart Hotel. It has certainly been around since 1729, when the vestry recorded that it had held a dinner there. The house was also used as a petty sessions court at the end of the 19th century.

WOODFORD BRIDGE
The Pond c1965 W479317

The first bridge was built in 1771 and a settlement soon grew up
around it. These flats beyond the ponds at Woodford Bridge were
built in about 1959, and changed this remoter part of the parish
from being what was generally described as a village into the
general conurbation of east London.

WOODFORD BRIDGE
The Pond and the Church c1965 W479318

St Paul's was established as an ecclesiastical parish, with its
original church, in 1854. That building was destroyed by fire
and replaced by the one we see here in 1886. It was designed
to seat 400 people.

▲ SOUTH WOODFORD
High Road c1965 S643009

This is Gladstone Terrace, built slightly before 1888. Broome's (left), the chemist's at the corner of Chelmsford Road and Derby Road, is a local landmark; their signboard declares that they have traded in the area since 1889. However, the building is absent on the Ordnance Survey map of the 1890s, and they only appear on this site in directories of the early 1900s.

▶ *detail from S643009*

SNARESBROOK
Eagle Pond 1903 50620B

Eagle Pond was named after the popular public house and one-time coaching
inn the Spread Eagle (substantially rebuilt as the Eagle). The area became very
popular with visitors from London after the establishment of the railway in 1856.
The common association of the pond with children relates to the 1843 building
of the Infant Orphan Asylum.

▼ **SOUTH WOODFORD,** *Gates Corner c1965* S643019

Frank Gates (left) had moved to this location by 1926 (having been in Chelmsford Road in 1922), and by 1937 was the main Ford dealer. There is a tendency to see the development of the London suburbs only in terms of public transport, but the motorcar proved increasingly important from this period. In the distance is the then Majestic Cinema. It was opened in 1934, and in the audience was a then less famous Winston Churchill. It was saved from redevelopment in the late 1990s after local protest.

► **SEVEN KINGS**
High Street c1955
S639006

To the extreme left of the photograph is the bus garage constructed by the London General Omnibus Company in 1913. Beyond that we can just see the sign of the Seven Kings Hotel. This had been the terminus for the bus company, and they virtually took over the drive of the Seven Kings Hotel.

CHADWELL HEATH
The Pavement 1908 60605

This is Blythswood Parade, constructed in the 1900s. It was built
as a consequence of the trams, which were established by Ilford
Urban District Council in 1903. The first two shops are a draper's
called Hone, and J Young, a confectioner.

COLLIER ROW
The Church of the Ascension 1908 59844

The chapel of the Ascension was built in 1882, and its first Vicar was the Reverend Joseph Hardwick Pemberton - he was still the Vicar when this photograph was taken. Considered then a part of Hainault Forest, Collier Row is now a sizeable conurbation.

SEVEN KINGS
Aldborough Road c1955
S639032

The Aldborough Road estates were established by the 1900s, and their own church of St John had been built by 1903. However, the Ordnance Survey maps surveyed shortly after the First World War show that the development had stopped short of this view. These shops were built around 1930.

FULLWELL CROSS
The Library 1967 F264014

This rather splendid piece of modernist architecture was constructed by the London Borough of Redbridge to designs by Sir Frederick Gibbard. It was reported to have a stock of 24,000 books. It was opened by the then Mayor Lionel Gooch in December 1967.

INDEX

Acknowledgements

No history is from scratch. Many hours were spent walking around checking the views, and talking to local residents, particularly Jaquie Upston of Harold Hill who helped me with the area around Havering-atte-Bower. Much of the information was taken from the histories of others. First, of course, there is the indispensable Victoria Country Histories, much of it for this area now on line (www.british-history.ac.uk), as well as the Buildings of England series by Nicolas Pevsner, and the Ordnance Survey 1:2500 1st edition (1860s), which has been reproduced on www.old-maps.co.uk. Then there are the photographic histories; 'Chigwell and Loughton' by Stephen Pewsy, for example, proved indispensable. I would also like to thank the staff at Local Studies and Archives in the London Borough of Redbridge, the county records office, and particularly the staff of Loughton Public Library.

NAMES OF SUBSCRIBERS

The following people have kindly supported this book by subscribing to copies before publication

Mr M Atwood

Susan Barnes, Chigwell

Sandra & Jade Berg, Molesey

James & Judith Bishop

Alec Borland

L G Bridgeman

Patricia Canes, Woodford Green, with love

Chigwell School

Mr & Mrs B Clarke

Paul Dalpe

Don from Anne, December 2004

Nick Flint

The Foster Family

Stephen & Clare Golding

Mr P Goracy

Mr T Gratton

Geoff Hamilton

K I Hughes

Ilford Old & New Series

The Ilford Recorder

Ian & Barbara Laidlaw, Chigwell Village

Gillian & Terence Leader and Robert Leader

Frank Leggatt

The Linney Family, Chigwell

The Loughton, Buckhurst Hill & Chigwell Guardian

The McLintock Family, once of Mamford Way

Mr & Mrs O L McMahon, Chigwell

George F Mace & Family, Buckhurst Hill

Henry, Joy, Clare, Paul & Nicola Mosely

Mr H Pearce

The Petchey Family, Chigwell Row

G H Prior

Mr Ron Porter

Gary Richards, Chigwell

The Roe Family, Buckhurst Hill

Timothy Ross

Mr O Sawyer

Harold, Ellen & Barry Schier

Nigel Sellens

The Shelly Family

Sheila Simmonds, Christmas 2004

Mrs Evelyn Storey

To Sylvia, 38 years in Chigwell, a token

Gerald Thake of Woodford Green

Keith & Kate Thomas

Graham Wakefield

Diane White

Kenneth Augustus Wilson

T A Wright

Robert & Morag Yorke

Frith Book Co Titles

www.francisfrith.co.uk

The Frith Book Company publishes over 100 new titles each year. A selection of those currentl available is listed below. For latest catalogue please contact Frith Book Co.

Town Books 96 pages, approximately 100 photos. *County and Themed Books* 128 pages, approximately 150 photos (unless specified). All titles hardback with laminated case and jacke except those indicated pb (paperback)

Title	ISBN	Price	Title	ISBN	Price
Amersham, Chesham & Rickmansworth (pb)	1-85937-340-2	£9.99	Devon (pb)	1-85937-297-x	£9.9
Andover (pb)	1-85937-292-9	£9.99	Devon Churches (pb)	1-85937-250-3	£9.9
Aylesbury (pb)	1-85937-227-9	£9.99	Dorchester (pb)	1-85937-307-0	£9.9
Barnstaple (pb)	1-85937-300-3	£9.99	Dorset (pb)	1-85937-269-4	£9.9
Basildon Living Memories (pb)	1-85937-515-4	£9.99	Dorset Coast (pb)	1-85937-299-6	£9.9
Bath (pb)	1-85937-419-0	£9.99	Dorset Living Memories (pb)	1-85937-584-7	£9.9
Bedford (pb)	1-85937-205-8	£9.99	Down the Severn (pb)	1-85937-560-x	£9.9
Bedfordshire Living Memories	1-85937-513-8	£14.99	Down The Thames (pb)	1-85937-278-3	£9.9
Belfast (pb)	1-85937-303-8	£9.99	Down the Trent	1-85937-311-9	£14.9
Berkshire (pb)	1-85937-191-4	£9.99	East Anglia (pb)	1-85937-265-1	£9.9
Berkshire Churches	1-85937-170-1	£17.99	East Grinstead (pb)	1-85937-138-8	£9.9
Berkshire Living Memories	1-85937-332-1	£14.99	East London	1-85937-080-2	£14.9
Black Country	1-85937-497-2	£12.99	East Sussex (pb)	1-85937-606-1	£9.9
Blackpool (pb)	1-85937-393-3	£9.99	Eastbourne (pb)	1-85937-399-2	£9.9
Bognor Regis (pb)	1-85937-431-x	£9.99	Edinburgh (pb)	1-85937-193-0	£8.9
Bournemouth (pb)	1-85937-545-6	£9.99	England In The 1880s	1-85937-331-3	£17.9
Bradford (pb)	1-85937-204-x	£9.99	Essex - Second Selection	1-85937-456-5	£14.9
Bridgend (pb)	1-85937-386-0	£7.99	Essex (pb)	1-85937-270-8	£9.9
Bridgwater (pb)	1-85937-305-4	£9.99	Essex Coast	1-85937-342-9	£14.9
Bridport (pb)	1-85937-327-5	£9.99	Essex Living Memories	1-85937-490-5	£14.9
Brighton (pb)	1-85937-192-2	£8.99	Exeter	1-85937-539-1	£9.9
Bristol (pb)	1-85937-264-3	£9.99	Exmoor (pb)	1-85937-608-8	£9.9
British Life A Century Ago (pb)	1-85937-213-9	£9.99	Falmouth (pb)	1-85937-594-4	£9.9
Buckinghamshire (pb)	1-85937-200-7	£9.99	Folkestone (pb)	1-85937-124-8	£9.9
Camberley (pb)	1-85937-222-8	£9.99	Frome (pb)	1-85937-317-8	£9.9
Cambridge (pb)	1-85937-422-0	£9.99	Glamorgan	1-85937-488-3	£14.9
Cambridgeshire (pb)	1-85937-420-4	£9.99	Glasgow (pb)	1-85937-190-6	£9.9
Cambridgeshire Villages	1-85937-523-5	£14.99	Glastonbury (pb)	1-85937-338-0	£7.9
Canals And Waterways (pb)	1-85937-291-0	£9.99	Gloucester (pb)	1-85937-232-5	£9.9
Canterbury Cathedral (pb)	1-85937-179-5	£9.99	Gloucestershire (pb)	1-85937-561-8	£9.9
Cardiff (pb)	1-85937-093-4	£9.99	Great Yarmouth (pb)	1-85937-426-3	£9.9
Carmarthenshire (pb)	1-85937-604-5	£9.99	Greater Manchester (pb)	1-85937-266-x	£9.9
Chelmsford (pb)	1-85937-310-0	£9.99	Guildford (pb)	1-85937-410-7	£9.9
Cheltenham (pb)	1-85937-095-0	£9.99	Hampshire (pb)	1-85937-279-1	£9.9
Cheshire (pb)	1-85937-271-6	£9.99	Harrogate (pb)	1-85937-423-9	£9.9
Chester (pb)	1-85937-382 8	£9.99	Hastings and Bexhill (pb)	1-85937-131-0	£9.9
Chesterfield (pb)	1-85937-378-x	£9.99	Heart of Lancashire (pb)	1-85937-197-3	£9.9
Chichester (pb)	1-85937-228-7	£9.99	Helston (pb)	1-85937-214-7	£9.9
Churches of East Cornwall (pb)	1-85937-249-x	£9.99	Hereford (pb)	1-85937-175-2	£9.9
Churches of Hampshire (pb)	1-85937-207-4	£9.99	Herefordshire (pb)	1-85937-567-7	£9.9
Cinque Ports & Two Ancient Towns	1-85937-492-1	£14.99	Herefordshire Living Memories	1-85937-514-6	£14.9
Colchester (pb)	1-85937-188-4	£8.99	Hertfordshire (pb)	1-85937-247-3	£9.9
Cornwall (pb)	1-85937-229-5	£9.99	Horsham (pb)	1-85937-432-8	£9.9
Cornwall Living Memories	1-85937-248-1	£14.99	Humberside (pb)	1-85937-605-3	£9.9
Cotswolds (pb)	1-85937-230-9	£9.99	Hythe, Romney Marsh, Ashford (pb)	1-85937-256-2	£9.9
Cotswolds Living Memories	1-85937-255-4	£14.99	Ipswich (pb)	1-85937-424-7	£9.9
County Durham (pb)	1-85937-398-4	£9.99	Isle of Man (pb)	1-85937-268-6	£9.9
Croydon Living Memories (pb)	1-85937-162-0	£9.99	Isle of Wight (pb)	1-85937-429-8	£9.9
Cumbria (pb)	1-85937-621-5	£9.99	Isle of Wight Living Memories	1-85937-304-6	£14.9
Derby (pb)	1-85937-367-4	£9.99	Kent (pb)	1-85937-189-2	£9.9
Derbyshire (pb)	1-85937-196-5	£9.99	Kent Living Memories(pb)	1-85937-401-8	£9.9
Derbyshire Living Memories	1-85937-330-5	£14.99	Kings Lynn (pb)	1-85937-334-8	£9.9

Available from your local bookshop or from the publisher

Frith Book Co Titles (continued)

Title	ISBN	Price	Title	ISBN	Price
ake District (pb)	1-85937-275-9	£9.99	Sherborne (pb)	1-85937-301-1	£9.99
ancashire Living Memories	1-85937-335-6	£14.99	Shrewsbury (pb)	1-85937-325-9	£9.99
ancaster, Morecambe, Heysham (pb)	1-85937-233-3	£9.99	Shropshire (pb)	1-85937-326-7	£9.99
eeds (pb)	1-85937-202-3	£9.99	Shropshire Living Memories	1-85937-643-6	£14.99
eicester (pb)	1-85937-381-x	£9.99	Somerset	1-85937-153-1	£14.99
eicestershire & Rutland Living Memories	1-85937-500-6	£12.99	South Devon Coast	1-85937-107-8	£14.99
eicestershire (pb)	1-85937-185-x	£9.99	South Devon Living Memories (pb)	1-85937-609-6	£9.99
ghthouses	1-85937-257-0	£9.99	South East London (pb)	1-85937-263-5	£9.99
ncoln (pb)	1-85937-380-1	£9.99	South Somerset	1-85937-318-6	£14.99
ncolnshire (pb)	1-85937-433-6	£9.99	South Wales	1-85937-519-7	£14.99
verpool and Merseyside (pb)	1-85937-234-1	£9.99	Southampton (pb)	1-85937-427-1	£9.99
ondon (pb)	1-85937-183-3	£9.99	Southend (pb)	1-85937-313-5	£9.99
ondon Living Memories	1-85937-454-9	£14.99	Southport (pb)	1-85937-425-5	£9.99
udlow (pb)	1-85937-176-0	£9.99	St Albans (pb)	1-85937-341-0	£9.99
uton (pb)	1-85937-235-x	£9.99	St Ives (pb)	1-85937-415-8	£9.99
Maidenhead (pb)	1-85937-339-9	£9.99	Stafford Living Memories (pb)	1-85937-503-0	£9.99
Maidstone (pb)	1-85937-391-7	£9.99	Staffordshire (pb)	1-85937-308-9	£9.99
Manchester (pb)	1-85937-198-1	£9.99	Stourbridge (pb)	1-85937-530-8	£9.99
Marlborough (pb)	1-85937-336-4	£9.99	Stratford upon Avon (pb)	1-85937-388-7	£9.99
Middlesex	1-85937-158-2	£14.99	Suffolk (pb)	1-85937-221-x	£9.99
Monmouthshire	1-85937-532-4	£14.99	Suffolk Coast (pb)	1-85937-610-x	£9.99
ew Forest (pb)	1-85937-390-9	£9.99	Surrey (pb)	1-85937-240-6	£9.99
ewark (pb)	1-85937-366-6	£9.99	Surrey Living Memories	1-85937-328-3	£14.99
ewport, Wales (pb)	1-85937-258-9	£9.99	Sussex (pb)	1-85937-184-1	£9.99
ewquay (pb)	1-85937-421-2	£9.99	Sutton (pb)	1-85937-337-2	£9.99
orfolk (pb)	1-85937-195-7	£9.99	Swansea (pb)	1-85937-167-1	£9.99
orfolk Broads	1-85937-486-7	£14.99	Taunton (pb)	1-85937-314-3	£9.99
orfolk Living Memories (pb)	1-85937-402-6	£9.99	Tees Valley & Cleveland (pb)	1-85937-623-1	£9.99
orth Buckinghamshire	1-85937-626-6	£14.99	Teignmouth (pb)	1-85937-370-4	£7.99
orth Devon Living Memories	1-85937-261-9	£14.99	Thanet (pb)	1-85937-116-7	£9.99
orth Hertfordshire	1-85937-547-2	£14.99	Tiverton (pb)	1-85937-178-7	£9.99
orth London (pb)	1-85937-403-4	£9.99	Torbay (pb)	1-85937-597-9	£9.99
orth Somerset	1-85937-302-x	£14.99	Truro (pb)	1-85937-598-7	£9.99
orth Wales (pb)	1-85937-298-8	£9.99	Victorian & Edwardian Dorset	1-85937-254-6	£14.99
orth Yorkshire (pb)	1-85937-236-8	£9.99	Victorian & Edwardian Kent (pb)	1-85937-624-X	£9.99
orthamptonshire Living Memories	1-85937-529-4	£14.99	Victorian & Edwardian Maritime Album (pb)	1-85937-622-3	£9.99
orthamptonshire	1-85937-150-7	£14.99	Victorian and Edwardian Sussex (pb)	1-85937-625-8	£9.99
orthumberland Tyne & Wear (pb)	1-85937-281-3	£9.99	Villages of Devon (pb)	1-85937-293-7	£9.99
orthumberland	1-85937-522-7	£14.99	Villages of Kent (pb)	1-85937-294-5	£9.99
orwich (pb)	1-85937-194-9	£8.99	Villages of Sussex (pb)	1-85937-295-3	£9.99
ottingham (pb)	1-85937-324-0	£9.99	Warrington (pb)	1-85937-507-3	£9.99
ottinghamshire (pb)	1-85937-187-6	£9.99	Warwick (pb)	1-85937-518-9	£9.99
xford (pb)	1-85937-411-5	£9.99	Warwickshire (pb)	1-85937-203-1	£9.99
xfordshire (pb)	1-85937-430-1	£9.99	Welsh Castles (pb)	1-85937-322-4	£9.99
xfordshire Living Memories	1-85937-525-1	£14.99	West Midlands (pb)	1-85937-289-9	£9.99
aignton (pb)	1-85937-374-7	£7.99	West Sussex (pb)	1-85937-607-x	£9.99
eak District (pb)	1-85937-280-5	£9.99	West Yorkshire (pb)	1-85937-201-5	£9.99
embrokeshire	1-85937-262-7	£14.99	Weston Super Mare (pb)	1-85937-306-2	£9.99
enzance (pb)	1-85937-595-2	£9.99	Weymouth (pb)	1-85937-209-0	£9.99
eterborough (pb)	1-85937-219-8	£9.99	Wiltshire (pb)	1-85937-277-5	£9.99
icturesque Harbours	1-85937-208-2	£14.99	Wiltshire Churches (pb)	1-85937-171-x	£9.99
iers	1-85937-237-6	£17.99	Wiltshire Living Memories (pb)	1-85937-396-8	£9.99
lymouth (pb)	1-85937-389-5	£9.99	Winchester (pb)	1-85937-428-x	£9.99
oole & Sandbanks (pb)	1-85937-251-1	£9.99	Windsor (pb)	1-85937-333-x	£9.99
reston (pb)	1-85937-212-0	£9.99	Wokingham & Bracknell (pb)	1-85937-329-1	£9.99
eading (pb)	1-85937-238-4	£9.99	Woodbridge (pb)	1-85937-498-0	£9.99
edhill to Reigate (pb)	1-85937-596-0	£9.99	Worcester (pb)	1-85937-165-5	£9.99
ingwood (pb)	1-85937-384-4	£7.99	Worcestershire Living Memories	1-85937-489-1	£14.99
omford (pb)	1-85937-319-4	£9.99	Worcestershire	1-85937-152-3	£14.99
oyal Tunbridge Wells (pb)	1-85937-504-9	£9.99	York (pb)	1-85937-199-x	£9.99
alisbury (pb)	1-85937-239-2	£9.99	Yorkshire	1-85937-186-8	£9.99
carborough (pb)	1-85937-379-8	£9.99	Yorkshire Coastal Memories	1-85937-506-5	£14.99
evenoaks and Tonbridge (pb)	1-85937-392-5	£9.99	Yorkshire Dales	1-85937-502-2	£14.99
heffield & South Yorks (pb)	1-85937-267-8	£9.99	Yorkshire Living Memories (pb)	1-85937-397-6	£9.99

See Frith books on the internet at www.francisfrith.co.uk

FRITH PRODUCTS & SERVICES

Francis Frith would doubtless be pleased to know that the pioneering publishing venture he started in 1860 still continues today. Over a hundred and forty years later, The Francis Frith Collection continues in the same innovative tradition and is now one of the foremost publishers of vintage photographs in the world. Some of the current activities include:

Interior Decoration

Today Frith's photographs can be seen framed and as giant wall murals in thousands of pubs, restaurants, hotels, banks, retail stores and other public buildings throughout the country. In every case they enhance the unique local atmosphere of the places they depict and provide reminders of gentler days in an increasingly busy and frenetic world.

Product Promotions

Frith products are used by many major companies to promote the sales of their own products or to reinforce their own history and heritage. Frith promotions have been used by Hovis bread, Courage beers, Scots Porage Oats, Colman's mustard, Cadbury's foods, Mellow Birds coffee, Dunhill pipe tobacco, Guinness, and Bulmer's Cider.

Genealogy and Family History

As the interest in family history and roots grows world-wide, more and more people are turning to Frith's photographs of Great Britain for images of the towns, villages and streets where their ancestors lived; and, of course, photographs of the churches and chapels where their ancestors were christened, married and buried are an essential part of every genealogy tree and family album.

Frith Products

All Frith photographs are available Framed or just as Mounted Prints and Posters (size 23 x 16 inches). These may be ordered from the address below. From time to time other products - Address Books, Calendars, Table Mats, etc - are available.

The Internet

Already fifty thousand Frith photographs can be viewed and purchased on the internet through the Frith websites and a myriad of partner sites.

For more detailed information on Frith companies and products, look at these sites:

www.francisfrith.co.uk
www.francisfrith.com
(for North American visitors)

See the complete list of Frith Books at:

www.francisfrith.co.uk

This web site is regularly updated with the latest list of publications from the Frith Book Company. If you wish to buy books relating to another part of the country that your local bookshop does not stock, you may purchase on-line.

For further information, trade, or author enquiries please contact us at the address below:
The Francis Frith Collection, Frith's Barn, Teffont, Salisbury, Wiltshire, England SP3 5QP.
Tel: +44 (0)1722 716 376 Fax: +44 (0)1722 716 881 Email: sales@francisfrith.co.uk

See Frith books on the internet at www.francisfrith.co.uk

FREE PRINT OF YOUR CHOICE

Mounted Print
Overall size 14 x 11 inches (355 x 280mm)

Choose any Frith photograph in this book.
Simply complete the Voucher opposite and return it with your remittance for £2.25 (to cover postage and handling) and we will print the photograph of your choice in SEPIA (size 11 x 8 inches) and supply it in a cream mount with a burgundy rule line (overall size 14 x 11 inches).
Please note: photographs with a reference number starting with a "Z" are not Frith photographs and cannot be supplied under this offer.
Offer valid for delivery to UK addresses only.

PLUS: Order additional Mounted Prints at HALF PRICE - £7.49 each (normally £14.99)
If you would like to order more Frith prints from this book, possibly as gifts for friends and family, you can buy them at half price (with no additional postage and handling costs).

PLUS: Have your Mounted Prints framed
For an extra £14.95 per print you can have your mounted print(s) framed in an elegant polished wood and gilt moulding, overall size 16 x 13 inches (no additional postage and handling required).

IMPORTANT!

These special prices are only available if you use this form to order. You must use the ORIGINAL VOUCHER on this page (no copies permitted). We can only despatch to one address. This offer cannot be combined with any other offer.

Send completed Voucher form to:
The Francis Frith Collection, Frith's Barn, Teffont, Salisbury, Wiltshire SP3 5QP

CHOOSE A PHOTOGRAPH FROM THIS BOOK

Voucher for **FREE** and Reduced Price Frith Prints

Please do not photocopy this voucher. Only the original is valid, so please fill it in, cut it out and return it to us with your order.

Picture ref no	Page no	Qty	Mounted @ £7.49	Framed + £14.95	Total Cost
		1	Free of charge*	£	£
			£7.49	£	£
			£7.49	£	£
			£7.49	£	£
			£7.49	£	£
			£7.49	£	£

Please allow 28 days for delivery

* Post & handling (UK)	£2.25
Total Order Cost	£

Title of this book . . . .
I enclose a cheque/postal order for £ . . . .
made payable to 'The Francis Frith Collection'

OR please debit my Mastercard / Visa / Switch (Maestro) /Amex card
(credit cards please on all overseas orders), details below

Card Number

Issue No (Switch only)   Valid from (Amex/Switch)

Expires   Signature

Name Mr/Mrs/Ms . . . .
Address . . . .
. . . .
. . . .
. . . . Postcode . . . .
Daytime Tel No . . . .
Email . . . .

Valid to 31/12/07

Would you like to find out more about Francis Frith?

We have recently recruited some entertaining speakers who are happy to visit local groups, clubs and societies to give an illustrated talk documenting Frith's travels and photographs. If you are a member of such a group and are interested in hosting a presentation, we would love to hear from you.

Our speakers bring with them a small selection of our local town and county books, together with sample prints. They are happy to take orders. A small proportion of the order value is donated to the group who have hosted the presentation. The talks are therefore an excellent way of fundraising for small groups and societies.

Can you help us with information about any of the Frith photographs in this book?

We are gradually compiling an historical record for each of the photographs in the Frith archive. It is always fascinating to find out the names of the people shown in the pictures, as well as insights into the shops, buildings and other features depicted.

If you recognize anyone in the photographs in this book, or if you have information not already included in the author's caption, do let us know. We would love to hear from you, and will try to publish it in future books or articles.

Our production team

Frith books are produced by a small dedicated team at offices in the converted Grade II listed 18th-century barn at Teffont near Salisbury, illustrated above. Most have worked with the Frith Collection for many years. All have in common one quality: they have a passion for the Frith Collection. The team is constantly expanding, but currently includes:

Paul Baron, Phillip Brennan, Jason Buck, John Buck, Ruth Butler, Heather Crisp, David Davies, Louis du Mont, Isobel Hall, Gareth Harris, Lucy Hart, Julian Hight, Peter Horne, James Kinnear, Karen Kinnear, Tina Leary, Stuart Login, David Marsh, Lesley-Ann Millard, Sue Molloy, Glenda Morgan, Wayne Morgan, Sarah Roberts, Kate Rotondetto, Dean Scource, Eliza Sackett, Terence Sackett, Sandra Sampson, Adrian Sanders, Sandra Sanger, Jan Scrivens, Julia Skinner, David Smith, Miles Smith, Lewis Taylor, Shelley Tolcher, Lorraine Tuck, Amanita Wainwright and Ricky Williams.

Free Print – see overleaf